EVELIN OIMANDI

Early Signs of Dementia and How to Beat It

Best Nordic Designs

First published by Best Nordic Designs 2023

Copyright © 2023 by Evelin Oimandi

All rights reserved. No part of this publication may be reproduced, stored or transmitted in any form or by any means, electronic, mechanical, photocopying, recording, scanning, or otherwise without written permission from the publisher. It is illegal to copy this book, post it to a website, or distribute it by any other means without permission.

First edition

This book was professionally typeset on Reedsy. Find out more at reedsy.com

Contents

Foreword	v
Introduction	vii
1 Chapter 1: Understanding Dementia	1
2 Chapter 2: Early Signs of Dementia	4
Memory Loss	4
Difficulty with Familiar Tasks	6
Confusion	7
Changes in Mood or Personality	9
Communication Problems	11
Difficulty with Spatial Awareness	12
3 Chapter 3: Diagnosing Dementia	16
The Diagnostic Process for Dementia	16
Medical History Review	18
Physical and Neurological Exams	20
Laboratory Tests	21
Imaging Studies	23
Cognitive Assessments	25
Diagnosing Different Types of Dementia	27
4 Chapter 4: Preventing Dementia	29
Exercise regularly	29
Maintain a healthy diet	30
Manage chronic health conditions	30
Stay socially active	30
Keep your brain active	31

	Get enough sleep	31
	Manage stress	31
5	Chapter 5: Managing Dementia	33
	Medications	33
	Cognitive Stimulation	35
	Exercise	37
	Nutrition	37
	Sleep	37
	Social Engagement	38
	Support for Caregivers	38
6	Chapter 6: Beating Dementia	40
	Stay Active	40
	Eat a Healthy Diet	43
	Engage in Mental Stimulation	44
	Get Enough Sleep	46
	Manage Stress	47
	Stay Socially Connected	49
	Seek Treatment for Health Conditions	50
7	Conclusion	54
Notes		57
About the Author		69
Also by Evelin Oimandi		70

Foreword

It is with great sadness and humility that I write this foreword for "Early Signs of Dementia and How to Beat It". My beloved grandmother, who I hold dear in my heart, was diagnosed with dementia a few years ago. As I watched her struggle with this illness, I realized how little I knew about it and how many misconceptions there were surrounding it.

Dementia is a complex and devastating disease that affects millions of people worldwide, and it can be difficult to recognize the early signs. In my grandmother's case, we noticed subtle changes in her behavior and memory that we attributed to old age. It was only after a thorough examination and assessment by a medical professional that we learned the truth.

Through this experience, I have learned the importance of recognizing the early signs of dementia and taking action as soon as possible. It is crucial to seek medical advice and support from family and friends to provide the best possible care for those who are affected by this disease.

This book provides valuable information on the early signs of dementia and how to beat it. It offers practical advice, tips, and strategies to help individuals and their loved ones manage the disease's challenges effectively. It is my sincere hope that this book will raise awareness about dementia and inspire others to take action to beat this disease.

I dedicate this book to my grandmother, who will always be a source of inspiration and love in my life, and to all the families who are affected by dementia.

Introduction

Dementia is a progressive neurological condition that affects memory, thinking, and behavior. It is a debilitating disorder that can significantly impact a person's ability to live independently and perform daily activities. While dementia is commonly associated with aging, it is not a normal part of the aging process. Dementia can affect people of all ages, and early detection is crucial for effective treatment and management.

Chapter 1: Understanding Dementia

In this chapter, we will explore what dementia is and its different types. We will also discuss the causes and risk factors associated with the disorder. Additionally, we will delve into the early signs of dementia and how it affects a person's life.

Chapter 2: Early Signs of Dementia

This chapter will focus on the early signs of dementia. We will discuss the changes that occur in a person's memory, thinking, and behavior. We will also talk about the difficulties that a person with dementia may face in their daily life, such as challenges with communication, mobility, and self-care.

Chapter 3: Diagnosing Dementia

In this chapter, we will talk about the diagnostic process for dementia. We will discuss the various assessments and tests that are used to diagnose the condition, including cognitive assessments, imaging tests, and blood tests.

Chapter 4: Preventing Dementia

In this chapter, we will explore the different ways to prevent or delay the onset of dementia. We will discuss lifestyle changes such as exercise, healthy eating habits, and social engagement. We will also talk about strategies to manage chronic health conditions that can increase the risk of dementia, such as diabetes and high blood pressure.

Chapter 5: Managing Dementia

This chapter will focus on the different approaches to managing dementia. We will discuss medications, therapies, and lifestyle changes that can help manage the symptoms of dementia. We will also explore different caregiving strategies and resources available for people with dementia and their families.

Chapter 6: Beating Dementia

In this final chapter, we will discuss strategies to beat dementia. We will talk about the latest research and advancements in dementia treatment, including emerging therapies and drugs. We will also explore the role of mental stimulation, social engagement, and physical activity in promoting brain health.

Conclusion

In conclusion, dementia is a complex neurological condition that affects millions of people worldwide. Early detection and diagnosis are critical to effective treatment and management. By understanding the early signs of dementia and adopting healthy lifestyle changes, we can prevent or delay its onset. With the right care and support, people with dementia can live meaningful lives and beat the condition.

1

Chapter 1: Understanding Dementia

Dementia is a term used to describe a group of symptoms associated with a decline in memory, thinking, and reasoning skills that can affect a person's ability to perform daily activities. It is a progressive condition that can become severe over time, ultimately leading to the loss of independence and the need for constant care.

Dementia is not a single disease but rather a term used to describe a range of conditions, including Alzheimer's disease, vascular dementia, frontotemporal dementia, Lewy body dementia, and others. These conditions share similar symptoms but differ in the underlying causes of the disease.

Although dementia is more commonly associated with aging, it is not a normal part of the aging process. Not everyone who ages will develop dementia, and not all types of dementia are related to age. In fact, some types of dementia can affect people as young as their 30s and 40s.[1]

The most common form of dementia is Alzheimer's disease, which accounts for 60-80% of all cases. Alzheimer's disease is a progressive disease that affects the brain, causing memory loss, difficulty with language, and a decline in other cognitive abilities. Other forms of dementia, such as vascular dementia, are caused by problems with blood flow to the brain, leading to damage to brain cells and a decline in cognitive abilities.[2]

The early signs of dementia can be subtle, and it can be challenging to differentiate them from normal age-related changes in cognitive abilities. Some early signs of dementia include forgetfulness, difficulty with familiar tasks, confusion, and personality changes.

If you or someone you love is experiencing these symptoms, it is essential to seek medical attention. While there is currently no cure for dementia, early intervention can help slow the progression of the disease and improve the quality of life for those affected by it.

There are also steps you can take to reduce your risk of developing dementia. These include maintaining a healthy diet and exercise routine, keeping your brain active through activities such as reading and puzzles, and managing any chronic health conditions, such as high blood pressure or diabetes, that can increase your risk of developing dementia.

In the following chapters of this book, we will explore the early signs of dementia in more detail and provide strategies for how to beat it. We will discuss lifestyle changes, such as diet and exercise, that can reduce your risk of developing dementia,

CHAPTER 1: UNDERSTANDING DEMENTIA

and explore ways to keep your brain active and engaged to maintain cognitive function as you age. We will also discuss the latest research and treatments for dementia, as well as provide guidance for caregivers who are supporting loved ones with dementia.

2

Chapter 2: Early Signs of Dementia

Dementia is a condition that affects the brain and can cause problems with memory, thinking, and behavior. While dementia is most commonly associated with older adults, it can occur in younger people as well. In this chapter, we will discuss some of the early signs of dementia and what to look out for.

Memory Loss

Memory loss is one of the most common early signs of dementia. This can manifest in a number of ways, such as forgetting recent events or conversations, losing track of personal belongings, or repeating questions or stories multiple times. It is important to note that occasional forgetfulness is normal, but frequent and persistent memory loss can be a cause for concern.

Memory loss is one of the hallmark symptoms of dementia,

CHAPTER 2: EARLY SIGNS OF DEMENTIA

which is a progressive neurological disorder that affects cognitive function, including memory, thinking, and behavior. According to the World Health Organization, dementia is a major public health issue affecting around 50 million people worldwide, with an estimated 10 million new cases every year[3]. Early detection and intervention are crucial to slowing the progression of the disease and improving the quality of life for those affected.

Memory loss can occur due to a variety of factors, including normal aging, stress, depression, and medical conditions such as Alzheimer's disease, which is the most common form of dementia. Alzheimer's disease is characterized by the buildup of abnormal proteins in the brain, which leads to the death of brain cells and a decline in cognitive function, including memory loss.[4]

There are different types of memory, including short-term memory, long-term memory, and working memory. Short-term memory refers to the ability to hold and recall information for a brief period, such as remembering a phone number. Long-term memory refers to the ability to store and retrieve information over a longer period, such as recalling events from one's childhood. Working memory refers to the ability to hold and manipulate information in the mind, such as mental arithmetic.

In the early stages of dementia, memory loss may be subtle and may affect short-term memory more than long-term memory. For example, a person may forget recent conversations or appointments but still remember events from their past.

As the disease progresses, memory loss may become more severe, affecting all types of memory and interfering with daily activities.

Difficulty with Familiar Tasks

Difficulty with familiar tasks is one of the early signs of dementia, which can be an alarming experience for both the individual and their loved ones. This symptom involves having difficulty completing everyday activities that the person has performed routinely throughout their life. Familiar tasks can range from personal hygiene, preparing meals, managing finances, and driving.

According to the Alzheimer's Association, this symptom is one of the most common and earliest signs of Alzheimer's disease, the most common form of dementia [4]. This difficulty arises from a combination of memory loss and impaired cognitive function. The individual may struggle with basic tasks, such as putting on clothes or brushing their teeth, because they cannot remember how to do it. They may also forget where they put their belongings, such as keys or glasses, and may have difficulty finding them.

Studies have shown that individuals with dementia may also struggle with more complex tasks, such as managing finances or using electronic devices[5]. These tasks require higher levels of cognitive function, such as problem-solving, attention, and executive function, which are all impaired in individuals with dementia.

Fortunately, there are strategies that individuals with dementia and their caregivers can use to cope with difficulty in familiar tasks. These include breaking down tasks into smaller steps, using visual aids, and creating a routine. Caregivers can also provide reminders and prompts to help the individual complete tasks.

It is important to note that difficulty with familiar tasks can also be caused by other conditions, such as depression or anxiety. Therefore, it is essential to consult a healthcare professional for a proper diagnosis and treatment plan.

In conclusion, difficulty with familiar tasks is a common and early sign of dementia. It can be distressing for both the individual and their loved ones, but there are strategies that can help them cope with the challenges. Early detection and treatment can also improve the individual's quality of life and delay the progression of the disease.

Confusion

People with dementia may become confused about time, place, and people. They may have trouble recognizing familiar faces or places, or become disoriented in their own home or neighborhood. This can lead to wandering, which can be dangerous, especially if the person becomes lost or disoriented.

Confusion is a common symptom of dementia and can be one of the earliest signs of cognitive decline[6]. It is a state of mind in which an individual experiences disorientation, difficulty in concentrating, and problems with memory recall. Confusion can lead to a sense of frustration, anxiety, and depression, making it challenging for individuals with dementia to carry out daily activities and interact with their environment.

The causes of confusion in dementia are complex and multifactorial. Some common factors that contribute to confusion in dementia include cognitive decline, sensory impairment, medication side effects, infections, and environmental changes[7]. As the disease progresses, the severity and frequency of confusion increase, making it difficult for caregivers and family members to manage the behavior of the person with dementia.

A study by Sampson et al.[8] found that individuals with Alzheimer's disease who experienced greater confusion were at a higher risk of functional decline and institutionalization. Similarly, a study by Seitz et al.[9] found that individuals with dementia who experienced greater confusion were at a higher risk of falls and hospitalization. These findings suggest that confusion is a significant risk factor for adverse outcomes in dementia.

However, there are strategies that can be used to manage confusion in dementia. According to the Alzheimer's Association, creating a consistent routine, simplifying the environment, and providing reassurance and comfort can help reduce confusion and improve the quality of life for individuals with dementia. Additionally, medication management and treating underlying medical conditions can also help reduce confusion in some cases.

In conclusion, confusion is a common symptom of dementia and can be one of the earliest signs of cognitive decline. It is a complex and multifactorial symptom that can lead to adverse outcomes in individuals with dementia. However, there are strategies that can be used to manage confusion in dementia and improve the quality of life for individuals with this disease.

Changes in Mood or Personality

Dementia can cause changes in mood and personality. People with dementia may become more anxious, irritable, or agitated than they were before. They may also become more withdrawn or depressed, or experience changes in their sense of humor or social behavior.

Changes in mood and personality can be early signs of dementia. Dementia is a term used to describe a group of symptoms that affect cognitive function, including memory loss, language difficulties, and impaired judgment. As the disease progresses, individuals may also experience changes in mood and personality, such as apathy, depression, irritability, and aggression.

One of the earliest signs of dementia is changes in mood and behavior. According to a study by the Alzheimer's Association, "changes in mood and behavior are often the first symptoms noticed by family members and caregivers"[10]. These changes can include a loss of interest in activities that were previously enjoyed, withdrawal from social situations, and difficulty in making decisions.

Another study conducted by the National Institute on Aging found that "changes in personality, such as becoming more suspicious or fearful, may be an early sign of dementia"[11]. In some cases, individuals may also exhibit increased anxiety, depression, or agitation.

It is important to note that changes in mood and personality can also be indicative of other medical conditions, such as depression or anxiety. Therefore, it is important to consult with a healthcare professional to receive a proper diagnosis.

If an individual is diagnosed with dementia, there are steps that can be taken to help manage the symptoms and slow the progression of the disease. One approach is to engage in activities that promote cognitive stimulation, such as puzzles or brain games. Another approach is to maintain a healthy diet and exercise regularly, as these can help improve brain function and overall health.

In conclusion, changes in mood and personality can be early signs of dementia. It is important to seek a proper diagnosis and to take steps to manage the symptoms and slow the progression of the disease. With early intervention and the right strategies, it is possible to beat this disease and improve overall quality of life.

CHAPTER 2: EARLY SIGNS OF DEMENTIA

Communication Problems

Communication problems are one of the early signs of dementia, and they can be very frustrating for both the person with dementia and their loved ones. Dementia is a progressive disease that affects cognitive functioning, including language and communication skills. As the disease progresses, people with dementia may experience difficulties in finding the right words, expressing themselves clearly, and understanding what others are saying.

Several studies have documented the impact of dementia on communication skills. A study by Fuh et al. (2006) found that people with dementia had difficulties in both expressive and receptive language. They had trouble recalling words and comprehending complex sentences. Another study by Green et al.[12] found that people with dementia had difficulties in initiating conversations and maintaining them. They also had trouble adjusting to changes in conversation topics.

These communication problems can lead to social isolation and a decrease in quality of life for the person with dementia. They may also lead to frustration and stress for caregivers and family members who may struggle to understand the person with dementia. Fortunately, there are strategies that can help to improve communication between the person with dementia and their loved ones.

One strategy is to use simple and concrete language. This can involve breaking down complex sentences into shorter ones and avoiding abstract concepts. It can also involve using gestures and facial expressions to support communication. Another strategy is to allow more time for the person with dementia to process information and respond. This can involve being patient and avoiding interrupting or finishing their sentences.

In conclusion, communication problems are one of the early signs of dementia and can be very challenging for both the person with dementia and their loved ones. However, there are strategies that can be used to improve communication and support social interactions. These strategies can include using simple and concrete language, allowing more time for the person with dementia to respond, and using non-verbal communication techniques.

Difficulty with Spatial Awareness

Dementia can also affect a person's ability to navigate their environment. They may have trouble judging distances or depth perception, and may become more prone to falls or accidents.

Difficulty with spatial awareness is a common early sign of dementia, particularly in the case of Alzheimer's disease[13]. Spatial awareness is the ability to understand and navigate the physical world around us. This includes judging distances, recognizing objects, and understanding the relationship between objects and space. Difficulty with spatial awareness can manifest in a variety of ways, including difficulty with depth perception, getting lost in familiar places, and difficulty with activities that require spatial awareness, such as reading a map or driving.

One study conducted by Geda et al.[14] found that difficulty with spatial awareness was one of the earliest signs of cognitive decline in individuals with Alzheimer's disease. The study found that individuals who experienced difficulty with spatial awareness were more likely to develop Alzheimer's disease than those who did not. Another study conducted by Iaria et al.[15] found that individuals with Alzheimer's disease showed significant impairment in spatial navigation tasks compared to healthy controls.

There are several reasons why difficulty with spatial awareness may occur in individuals with dementia. One theory is that damage to the hippocampus, a part of the brain that plays a critical role in spatial awareness and memory, may be responsible for this symptom[16]. Another theory is that damage to the parietal lobe, which is involved in processing spatial information, may also contribute to difficulty with spatial awareness in individuals with dementia[15].

It is important to note that difficulty with spatial awareness is not always indicative of dementia. Other conditions, such as visual impairments, can also contribute to difficulty with spatial awareness. However, if an individual is experiencing difficulty with spatial awareness in conjunction with other early signs of dementia, such as memory loss or difficulty with language, it is important to seek medical attention.

In conclusion, difficulty with spatial awareness is a common early sign of dementia, particularly in individuals with Alzheimer's disease. This symptom can manifest in a variety of ways and may be caused by damage to the hippocampus or parietal lobe. If an individual is experiencing difficulty with spatial awareness in conjunction with other early signs of dementia, it is important to seek medical attention.

It is important to note that not all of these symptoms will necessarily be present in every person with dementia, and some symptoms may be more pronounced than others. However, if you or someone you know is experiencing any of these early signs of dementia, it is important to seek medical attention as soon as possible.

CHAPTER 2: EARLY SIGNS OF DEMENTIA

3

Chapter 3: Diagnosing Dementia

Dementia is a complex condition that can be difficult to diagnose, as there are many different types and causes of dementia. In this chapter, we will explore the diagnostic process for dementia and the tests and assessments used to diagnose the condition.

The Diagnostic Process for Dementia

The diagnostic process for dementia involves a thorough evaluation of an individual's cognitive and functional abilities. It typically involves a combination of medical history, physical examination, cognitive and neuropsychological testing, laboratory tests, and imaging studies. This process aims to identify the underlying cause of cognitive impairment and determine the type and severity of dementia.

CHAPTER 3: DIAGNOSING DEMENTIA

According to the Alzheimer's Association[17], the diagnostic process for dementia involves several steps. First, a healthcare provider will conduct a medical history interview to gather information about the individual's symptoms, medical conditions, medications, and family history of dementia. This information can help identify potential risk factors or underlying medical conditions that may contribute to cognitive impairment.

Second, a physical examination is conducted to assess overall health and identify any medical conditions that may be contributing to cognitive impairment. This may involve a neurological exam to assess reflexes, strength, coordination, and sensation.

Third, cognitive and neuropsychological testing may be conducted to evaluate memory, attention, language, executive function, and other cognitive abilities. These tests can help identify patterns of cognitive impairment and rule out other conditions that may mimic dementia.

Fourth, laboratory tests may be ordered to assess blood sugar levels, thyroid function, vitamin B12 levels, and other biomarkers that may indicate an underlying medical condition contributing to cognitive impairment.

Finally, imaging studies such as magnetic resonance imaging (MRI) or computed tomography (CT) scans may be ordered to assess brain structure and identify any abnormalities that may be contributing to cognitive impairment.

The diagnostic process for dementia can be complex and

time-consuming, and it may require input from a team of healthcare professionals, including neurologists, geriatricians, neuropsychologists, and other specialists. However, an accurate diagnosis is crucial for providing appropriate treatment and support to individuals with dementia.

Early diagnosis of dementia is important, as it allows for earlier intervention and management of symptoms. There are also potential benefits for individuals and their families, such as access to support services, financial planning, and the opportunity to participate in clinical trials of new treatments.

Medical History Review

The first step in diagnosing dementia is usually a review of the patient's medical history. The doctor will ask the patient about their symptoms, when they began, and how they have progressed over time. The doctor will also ask about the patient's family history, any medical conditions they have, and any medications they are taking.

Medical history review is an essential component of the diagnostic process for any medical condition, including dementia. When evaluating patients for possible dementia, a detailed medical history can provide valuable information about potential risk factors, the course of the disease, and response to treatment.

CHAPTER 3: DIAGNOSING DEMENTIA

Several studies have shown that certain medical conditions are associated with an increased risk of developing dementia, such as hypertension, diabetes, and cardiovascular disease[18] [19]. Therefore, a review of a patient's medical history should include a thorough assessment of these conditions, including past treatments and current medications.

In addition to medical conditions, lifestyle factors such as diet, exercise, and smoking can also impact the risk of dementia[19]. A medical history review should include questions about these factors to identify potential areas for intervention to reduce risk or slow disease progression.

Other factors that may be relevant to a medical history review for dementia include a family history of the disease, past head injuries, and psychiatric history[19]. These factors can provide important clues about the underlying causes of the patient's cognitive decline.

In summary, a thorough medical history review is an important component of the diagnostic process for dementia. By evaluating a patient's medical history, clinicians can identify potential risk factors, tailor treatment plans to the patient's specific needs, and develop strategies for slowing disease progression.

Physical and Neurological Exams

After the medical history review, the doctor will perform a physical exam to assess the patient's overall health. This will include checking their blood pressure, heart rate, and other vital signs, as well as examining their eyes, ears, nose, and throat.

The doctor will also perform a neurological exam to assess the patient's cognitive function, coordination, reflexes, and other neurological functions. This may involve asking the patient to perform certain tasks, such as counting backwards from 100, recalling a list of words, or touching their nose with their finger.

Physical and neurological exams are critical components in the assessment of individuals with suspected dementia. The physical exam is used to identify any underlying medical conditions that may be contributing to cognitive impairment, such as thyroid dysfunction or vitamin deficiencies[20]. Meanwhile, the neurological exam is used to evaluate brain function, such as memory, language, and visual-spatial skills[21].

The physical exam typically includes a review of medical history, vital signs, and a comprehensive physical assessment. For example, a thorough examination of the heart, lungs, and abdominal organs may be performed to rule out any cardiovascular or gastrointestinal conditions that may cause cognitive symptoms. Additionally, a detailed neurological exam should be conducted to assess the individual's gait, muscle tone, reflexes, and sensory function[22].

The neurological exam is particularly important for detecting early signs of dementia. The exam should evaluate multiple cognitive domains, including memory, language, attention, executive function, and visuospatial abilities[23]. Tests such as the Mini-Mental State Examination (MMSE) and the Montreal Cognitive Assessment (MoCA) are commonly used to assess cognitive function[21].

Research has shown that combining physical and neurological exams can improve the accuracy of diagnosing dementia. In a study by Triebel et al.[24], it was found that incorporating a physical exam into a dementia evaluation increased the diagnostic accuracy from 71% to 83%. Furthermore, the neurological exam helped to differentiate dementia from other conditions that may mimic cognitive impairment, such as depression or anxiety[24].

In conclusion, physical and neurological exams are crucial in identifying early signs of dementia and ruling out other medical conditions that may be contributing to cognitive impairment. Combining these exams can improve diagnostic accuracy and lead to more effective treatments for individuals with dementia.

Laboratory Tests

Laboratory tests may be performed to help diagnose dementia and rule out other conditions that may cause similar symptoms. These tests may include blood tests, urine tests, and other tests to assess the patient's overall health.

Dementia is a neurodegenerative disease that affects a person's cognitive abilities, behavior, and memory. It is a growing concern in the aging population, and early detection is crucial to ensure that patients receive appropriate treatment and care. Laboratory tests are an important tool in the diagnostic process of dementia.

Blood tests can help to identify potential causes of dementia, such as thyroid disorders, vitamin deficiencies, and infections. A study by de Bruijn et al.[25] found that low vitamin B12 levels were associated with an increased risk of dementia. Additionally, certain blood tests can detect genetic markers that increase a person's risk of developing Alzheimer's disease, such as the APOE4 gene[26].

Imaging tests, such as magnetic resonance imaging (MRI) and positron emission tomography (PET), can provide detailed images of the brain and help to identify structural changes or abnormal activity patterns that are associated with dementia. A study by Mattsson et al.[27] found that PET scans can detect beta-amyloid plaques in the brain, which are a hallmark of Alzheimer's disease.

Cerebrospinal fluid (CSF) tests can also provide valuable information about the presence of beta-amyloid and tau proteins, which are indicative of Alzheimer's disease. A study by Olsson et al.[28] found that CSF biomarkers were able to accurately predict the progression of mild cognitive impairment to dementia.

While laboratory tests can provide important information in the diagnostic process of dementia, they should be used in conjunction with other diagnostic tools, such as cognitive assessments and patient history. Additionally, it is important to note that laboratory tests alone cannot diagnose dementia, and a comprehensive evaluation by a healthcare professional is necessary.

In conclusion, laboratory tests are an essential component of the diagnostic process for dementia. Blood tests, imaging tests, and CSF tests can provide valuable information about potential causes of dementia and help to identify structural and biochemical changes in the brain. It is important to use laboratory tests in conjunction with other diagnostic tools and to seek a comprehensive evaluation by a healthcare professional.

Imaging Studies

Imaging studies, such as magnetic resonance imaging (MRI) or computed tomography (CT) scans, may also be used to diagnose dementia. These imaging tests can help detect abnormalities in the brain, such as shrinkage or damage to certain areas.

Imaging studies play a crucial role in the early detection and diagnosis of dementia. Several types of imaging techniques, including structural and functional imaging, are used to evaluate the brain changes that occur in dementia patients.

Structural imaging techniques, such as magnetic resonance imaging (MRI) and computed tomography (CT), are used to visualize the structure of the brain and detect any abnormalities. For instance, studies have shown that MRI can detect hippocampal atrophy, which is a hallmark of Alzheimer's disease, in its early stages[29]. CT scans can also detect structural abnormalities such as ventricular enlargement, which is common in patients with dementia[30].

Functional imaging techniques, such as positron emission tomography (PET) and single-photon emission computed tomography (SPECT), are used to evaluate the metabolic and physiological changes that occur in the brain. For example, studies have shown that PET can detect changes in glucose metabolism in the brain, which can help differentiate Alzheimer's disease from other forms of dementia[31]. SPECT imaging can also be used to measure regional cerebral blood flow, which is useful in evaluating vascular dementia[32].

In addition to structural and functional imaging, there are emerging techniques such as diffusion tensor imaging (DTI) and functional magnetic resonance imaging (fMRI), which can provide more detailed information about the brain's white matter tracts and functional connectivity, respectively. These techniques are still under investigation for their utility in the diagnosis of dementia[33].

Imaging studies are critical for the early detection and diagnosis of dementia. They can detect brain changes before symptoms appear, which can lead to earlier intervention and better outcomes for patients. However, it is important to note that imaging studies should not be used in isolation and should always be interpreted in conjunction with a clinical assessment.

Cognitive Assessments

Cognitive assessments are important tools for identifying the early signs of dementia and for monitoring the progression of the disease. These assessments are used to evaluate a person's cognitive abilities, including their memory, language, attention, and executive function.

One commonly used cognitive assessment tool is the Mini-Mental State Examination (MMSE), which has been widely used for more than 40 years to assess cognitive impairment. The MMSE includes questions related to orientation, attention, memory, language, and visuospatial skills. The maximum score is 30, with scores of 24 or below indicating cognitive impairment.[34]

Another cognitive assessment tool is the Montreal Cognitive Assessment (MoCA), which is a more sensitive tool for detecting early cognitive impairment. The MoCA assesses cognitive domains such as attention, concentration, executive functions, memory, language, visuospatial skills, conceptual thinking, calculations, and orientation. The maximum score is 30, with scores below 26 indicating cognitive impairment.[35]

Research has shown that cognitive assessments can be effective in identifying early signs of dementia. For example, a study by Proust-Lima et al.[36] found that cognitive assessments can predict dementia up to 10 years before diagnosis. Another study by Ossenkoppele et al.[37] found that cognitive assessments, along with other biomarkers, can accurately predict the risk of dementia in people with mild cognitive impairment.

Cognitive assessments are also useful in monitoring the progression of dementia. Regular assessments can help healthcare professionals to identify changes in cognitive function and adjust treatment plans accordingly. A study by Rodriguez-Gomez et al.[38] found that regular cognitive assessments can help to improve the accuracy of dementia diagnosis and reduce the time to diagnosis.

In conclusion, cognitive assessments are important tools for identifying the early signs of dementia and for monitoring the progression of the disease. The MMSE and MoCA are commonly used cognitive assessment tools, and research has shown that they can be effective in predicting the risk of dementia and in monitoring the progression of the disease. Regular cognitive assessments can help to improve the accuracy of dementia diagnosis and allow for timely intervention and treatment.

CHAPTER 3: DIAGNOSING DEMENTIA

Diagnosing Different Types of Dementia

There are many different types of dementia, and the diagnostic process may vary depending on the type of dementia suspected.

Alzheimer's disease, the most common type of dementia, is typically diagnosed based on a combination of medical history review, physical and neurological exams, laboratory tests, imaging studies, and cognitive assessments. However, a definitive diagnosis of Alzheimer's disease can only be made after a postmortem examination of the brain.[39]

Vascular dementia, which is caused by reduced blood flow to the brain, may be diagnosed based on a history of stroke or cardiovascular disease, as well as imaging studies that show evidence of brain damage.[40]

Lewy body dementia, which is characterized by abnormal protein deposits in the brain, may be diagnosed based on a combination of cognitive assessments, physical and neurological exams, and imaging studies that show evidence of Lewy bodies in the brain.[41]

Frontotemporal dementia, which affects the frontal and temporal lobes of the brain, may be diagnosed based on changes in personality and behavior, as well as cognitive assessments that show deficits in language and executive function.[42]

Conclusion

Diagnosing dementia is a complex process that requires a careful evaluation of a patient's medical history, physical and neurological function, laboratory tests, imaging studies, and cognitive assessments. Early diagnosis is critical for ensuring that patients receive appropriate treatment and care, and can help improve their quality of life and overall well being.

4

Chapter 4: Preventing Dementia

Dementia is a debilitating condition that affects many people as they age. While there is no cure for dementia, there are steps that individuals can take to prevent it from developing. In this chapter, we will explore some of the ways that you can reduce your risk of developing dementia and maintain a healthy brain throughout your life.

Exercise regularly

Exercise is essential for maintaining good physical and mental health. Regular exercise can help to improve blood flow to the brain, reduce inflammation, and promote the growth of new brain cells[43]. Aim to get at least 150 minutes of moderate-intensity exercise each week, such as brisk walking, cycling, or swimming.

Maintain a healthy diet

A healthy diet is crucial for maintaining good brain health. Eat a balanced diet that is rich in fruits, vegetables, whole grains, lean proteins, and healthy fats such as omega-3 fatty acids. Avoid excessive alcohol consumption, as this can damage the brain and increase the risk of dementia.[44]

Manage chronic health conditions

Chronic health conditions such as diabetes, high blood pressure, and high cholesterol can increase the risk of developing dementia.[45] Take steps to manage these conditions by following your doctor's recommendations for medication, diet, and exercise.

Stay socially active

Social interaction is important for maintaining good mental health and cognitive function[46]. Stay connected with friends and family, join social clubs or organizations, and volunteer in your community.

Keep your brain active

Engaging in mentally stimulating activities can help to improve cognitive function and reduce the risk of dementia. Activities such as reading, solving puzzles, playing games, and learning a new language or skill can all help to keep your brain active and healthy.[47]

Get enough sleep

Sleep is essential for good mental and physical health. Aim to get 7-9 hours of sleep each night, and establish a regular sleep routine to ensure that you get enough restful sleep.[48]

Manage stress

Chronic stress can have negative effects on both physical and mental health, including increasing the risk of dementia.[49] Take steps to manage stress, such as practicing relaxation techniques, getting regular exercise, and seeking support from friends, family, or a mental health professional.

In conclusion, there are several steps that you can take to reduce your risk of developing dementia and maintain a healthy brain throughout your life. By following these recommendations for regular exercise, a healthy diet, managing chronic health conditions, staying socially active, keeping your brain active, getting enough sleep, and managing stress, you can reduce your risk of developing dementia and enjoy a healthy and fulfilling life.

5

Chapter 5: Managing Dementia

Dementia is a progressive disease, which means that it gradually gets worse over time. However, there are ways to manage the symptoms and slow down the progression of the disease. In this chapter, we will explore various strategies that can help individuals with dementia and their caregivers.

Medications

There are several medications available that can help manage the symptoms of dementia. These medications work by increasing the levels of certain chemicals in the brain that are involved in memory and cognition. They can improve memory, thinking, and behavior in some people with dementia. However, these medications do not cure the disease and do not work for everyone.

Medications are an important component of the treatment plan for dementia. They can help manage symptoms, slow down the progression of the disease, and improve quality of life for those living with dementia. There are several types of medications that are commonly used in the treatment of dementia, including cholinesterase inhibitors, memantine, and antidepressants[50].

Cholinesterase inhibitors are medications that work by increasing the levels of a chemical called acetylcholine in the brain. This chemical is important for memory and learning, and is often depleted in individuals with dementia. Studies have shown that cholinesterase inhibitors can improve cognitive function and reduce behavioral symptoms in people with mild to moderate Alzheimer's disease[51]. Some examples of cholinesterase inhibitors include donepezil, rivastigmine, and galantamine[52].

Memantine is another medication that is commonly used in the treatment of dementia. It works by blocking a chemical called glutamate, which is responsible for the death of brain cells in people with Alzheimer's disease. Studies have shown that memantine can improve cognitive function and reduce behavioral symptoms in people with moderate to severe Alzheimer's disease[53].

Antidepressants are sometimes used in the treatment of dementia, particularly in cases where the individual is experiencing depression or anxiety. These medications can help improve mood and reduce agitation, and may also improve cognitive function in some individuals[54]. However, it is important to note that antidepressants may have side effects and should only be used under the supervision of a healthcare professional.

In addition to these medications, there are also several non-pharmacological interventions that can help manage symptoms of dementia. These may include cognitive stimulation therapy, physical exercise, and social engagement[55]. It is important for individuals with dementia and their caregivers to work closely with healthcare professionals to develop a comprehensive treatment plan that includes both medications and non-pharmacological interventions[56].

Cognitive Stimulation

Cognitive stimulation involves engaging in activities that challenge the brain, such as crossword puzzles, word games, and memory exercises. This can help maintain cognitive function and slow down the progression of the disease[57]. It is important to find activities that are enjoyable and stimulating for the individual with dementia.

Cognitive stimulation is a powerful tool for individuals with early signs of dementia. It involves activities and exercises that are designed to engage the brain, stimulate mental activity, and maintain cognitive abilities. Research has shown that cognitive stimulation can improve memory, language, attention, and overall cognitive function in people with dementia[58]. In this chapter, we will explore the benefits of cognitive stimulation and provide examples of activities that can be incorporated into a daily routine.

One of the key benefits of cognitive stimulation is that it can slow down the progression of dementia[59]. Studies have shown that engaging in cognitive stimulation activities can delay the onset of cognitive decline and reduce the risk of developing dementia[60]. Cognitive stimulation also has a positive impact on mood and quality of life, which is important for individuals with dementia and their caregivers[61].

There are many different types of cognitive stimulation activities that can be incorporated into a daily routine. Some examples include crossword puzzles, reading, playing board games, learning a new language, and engaging in social activities. It is important to choose activities that are enjoyable and challenging but not too difficult, as this can cause frustration and reduce motivation[58].

In addition to traditional cognitive stimulation activities, there are also specialized programs that are designed specifically for individuals with dementia. For example, cognitive stimulation therapy (CST) is a program that involves structured activities and exercises that target different areas of cognitive function, such as memory, attention, and language[62]. CST has been shown to improve cognitive function and quality of life in individuals with dementia[63].

In conclusion, cognitive stimulation is an effective tool for individuals with early signs of dementia. It can slow down the progression of cognitive decline, improve cognitive function, and enhance quality of life. By incorporating cognitive stimulation activities into a daily routine, individuals with dementia can maintain their cognitive abilities and continue to engage with the world around them.

Exercise

Regular exercise can help improve overall health and well-being in people with dementia[64]. Exercise can also help reduce the risk of developing other health conditions, such as heart disease and diabetes. Physical activity can also improve mood and reduce stress, which can be beneficial for individuals with dementia.

Nutrition

A healthy diet is important for everyone, but it is especially important for individuals with dementia. Eating a diet rich in fruits, vegetables, whole grains, and lean proteins can help improve overall health and well-being. It is important to avoid foods that are high in saturated and trans fats, as well as sugary and processed foods.[65]

Sleep

Getting enough sleep is important for overall health and well-being, but it can be difficult for individuals with dementia. Sleep disturbances are common in people with dementia, and they can exacerbate other symptoms of the disease. It is important to establish a regular sleep routine and create a comfortable sleep environment.[66]

Social Engagement

Social engagement can help improve mood and reduce stress in individuals with dementia[67]. It is important to encourage social activities, such as spending time with friends and family, participating in group activities, and attending social events. Social engagement can also help maintain cognitive function and slow down the progression of the disease.

Support for Caregivers

Caring for someone with dementia can be challenging and stressful. It is important for caregivers to take care of themselves and seek support when needed. This can include seeking respite care, attending support groups, and accessing community resources. Caregivers should also make time for self-care activities, such as exercise, relaxation, and social activities.

In conclusion, managing dementia involves a multifaceted approach that includes medications, cognitive stimulation, exercise, nutrition, sleep, social engagement, and support for caregivers. These strategies can help improve overall health

CHAPTER 5: MANAGING DEMENTIA

and well-being in individuals with dementia and slow down the progression of the disease. It is important to work with healthcare professionals to develop a personalized plan for managing dementia.

6

Chapter 6: Beating Dementia

Dementia is a devastating disease that affects millions of people around the world. It is a progressive condition that causes a decline in cognitive function, memory loss, and personality changes. While there is currently no cure for dementia, there are steps that you can take to reduce your risk of developing the condition and to slow its progression if you have already been diagnosed. In this chapter, we will explore some of the ways in which you can beat dementia.

Stay Active

One of the best ways to beat dementia is to stay physically active[68]. Regular exercise can help to improve blood flow to the brain, which is essential for maintaining cognitive function. It can also help to reduce the risk of developing conditions that can increase the risk of dementia, such as high blood pressure and diabetes. Aim to engage in at least 30 minutes of moderate-intensity exercise most days of the week.[69]

Dementia is a progressive cognitive decline that affects various cognitive abilities, such as memory, language, attention, and problem-solving[70]. According to the World Health Organization (WHO), there are about 50 million people living with dementia worldwide, and this number is expected to triple by 2050. Although there is no known cure for dementia, early detection and intervention can help manage the symptoms and improve the quality of life. One of the ways to reduce the risk of dementia is to stay physically and mentally active.

Physical activity is defined as any bodily movement produced by skeletal muscles that results in energy expenditure. Several studies have shown that physical activity is associated with a reduced risk of dementia. For instance, a meta-analysis of 20 studies found that physical activity was associated with a 28% reduced risk of developing dementia[71]. Moreover, a randomized controlled trial of 1,260 sedentary older adults found that a 24-month physical activity intervention was associated with a significant improvement in cognitive function compared to a health education program[72]. These findings suggest that physical activity is a viable strategy to prevent or delay the onset of dementia.

Mental activity refers to cognitive stimulation, such as reading, writing, playing games, and learning new skills. Several studies have shown that mental activity is associated with a reduced risk of dementia. For instance, a systematic review of 15 studies found that cognitive activity was associated with a 38% reduced risk of developing dementia[73]. Moreover, a randomized controlled trial of 2,802 older adults found that a computerized cognitive training program was associated with a significant improvement in cognitive function compared to a control group[74]. These findings suggest that mental activity is also a viable strategy to prevent or delay the onset of dementia.

Several studies have suggested that a combination of physical and mental activity may have a synergistic effect on reducing the risk of dementia. For instance, a randomized controlled trial of 1,584 older adults found that a 6-month program that combined physical activity and cognitive training was associated with a significant improvement in cognitive function compared to a health education program[75]. Another randomized controlled trial of 126 sedentary older adults found that a 24-month program that combined physical activity and cognitive training was associated with a significant improvement in cognitive function compared to a health education program[76]. These findings suggest that a combination of physical and mental activity may be the most effective strategy to prevent or delay the onset of dementia.

In conclusion, staying physically and mentally active is a viable strategy to prevent or delay the onset of dementia. Physical activity, mental activity, and a combination of physical and mental activity have all been shown to be effective in reducing the risk of dementia. Therefore, it is essential to encourage older adults to engage in regular physical and mental activities to maintain their cognitive health and improve their quality of life.

Eat a Healthy Diet

Diet plays a significant role in brain health, and consuming a healthy diet can help to reduce the risk of developing dementia[77]. A diet rich in fruits, vegetables, whole grains, lean protein, and healthy fats can provide the nutrients necessary for optimal brain function. Try to avoid processed and sugary foods, which can increase inflammation in the body and contribute to cognitive decline.[78]

Maintaining a healthy diet is crucial in reducing the risk of developing dementia. A study conducted by Xu et al.[79] found that adherence to a healthy diet was associated with a lower risk of cognitive decline and dementia. In contrast, a diet high in saturated and trans fats, processed meats, and added sugars has been linked to an increased risk of cognitive impairment[80].

The Mediterranean diet, which is rich in fruits, vegetables, whole grains, nuts, legumes, and healthy fats, has been consistently associated with a reduced risk of dementia and cognitive decline[81]. This diet also promotes cardiovascular health and reduces the risk of other chronic diseases, such as diabetes and hypertension, which have been linked to cognitive impairment[82].

Moreover, certain nutrients have been found to be particularly beneficial for brain health. Omega-3 fatty acids, found in fatty fish, nuts, and seeds, have been associated with a lower risk of dementia[83]. Vitamin E, found in nuts, seeds, and leafy greens, has also been linked to a reduced risk of cognitive decline[84].

In addition to a healthy diet, maintaining a healthy weight and engaging in regular physical activity can also reduce the risk of dementia[85]. A study by Norton et al. (2014) found that individuals with a body mass index (BMI) in the overweight or obese range had a higher risk of dementia compared to those with a healthy BMI[86]. Exercise has been shown to improve cognitive function and reduce the risk of cognitive decline[87].

In conclusion, a healthy diet, particularly one that follows the principles of the Mediterranean diet, can help reduce the risk of dementia and cognitive decline. Consuming omega-3 fatty acids and vitamin E can also be beneficial for brain health. Additionally, maintaining a healthy weight and engaging in regular physical activity can further reduce the risk of developing dementia.

Engage in Mental Stimulation

Regular mental stimulation is essential for maintaining cognitive function and reducing the risk of dementia. Activities that challenge the brain, such as crossword puzzles, Sudoku, and reading, can help to keep the mind sharp. You can also try learning a new skill or language to keep your brain engaged.[88]

Engaging in mental stimulation has been shown to be an effective way to reduce the risk of developing dementia and to help slow its progression in individuals who already have the condition[89]. Studies have demonstrated that mental stimulation can improve cognitive function and protect against brain

CHAPTER 6: BEATING DEMENTIA

deterioration, which are important factors in reducing the risk of developing dementia[90].

One study found that older adults who engaged in mentally stimulating activities, such as reading, doing puzzles, and playing games, had a reduced risk of developing dementia compared to those who did not engage in such activities[91]. Another study showed that mental stimulation can help slow the progression of dementia in individuals who already have the condition[92].

There are several reasons why mental stimulation is believed to be beneficial for brain health. One theory is that mental stimulation increases the production of brain-derived neurotrophic factor (BDNF), which is a protein that helps to support the growth and survival of neurons in the brain[93]. Other research suggests that mental stimulation can improve the function of the brain's frontal lobe, which is involved in cognitive processes such as attention, memory, and problem-solving[94].

Engaging in mental stimulation can take many forms, and the key is to find activities that are challenging and enjoyable. Some examples of mentally stimulating activities include reading, writing, doing crossword puzzles, playing board games, learning a new language, and engaging in creative activities such as painting or music.

In conclusion, engaging in mental stimulation is an effective way to reduce the risk of developing dementia and to help slow its progression in individuals who already have the condition. There are many different ways to engage in mental stimulation, and it is important to find activities that are both challenging and enjoyable. By incorporating mental stimulation into our daily lives, we can help protect our brains and maintain cognitive function as we age.

Get Enough Sleep

Getting enough sleep is essential for overall health and well-being, including cognitive function. In fact, studies have shown that chronic sleep deprivation may increase the risk of developing dementia and other cognitive disorders[95]. It is recommended that adults aim for 7-9 hours of sleep per night to maintain optimal cognitive health[96].

Sleep is essential for the consolidation of memories and the removal of waste products from the brain, such as beta-amyloid, which is a hallmark of Alzheimer's disease[97]. Chronic sleep deprivation can lead to an accumulation of beta-amyloid and other toxins in the brain, which can contribute to cognitive decline[98].

Additionally, lack of sleep can impair executive function, attention, and working memory, which are all critical cognitive processes necessary for daily functioning and decision-making[99]. Poor sleep quality has also been linked to an increased risk of developing depression and anxiety, which can further impact cognitive health[100].

To ensure adequate sleep, individuals should establish a consistent sleep schedule and practice good sleep hygiene, such as avoiding caffeine and alcohol before bed and creating a comfortable sleep environment[101]. In cases where sleep disturbances persist, individuals should consult with a healthcare provider to rule out underlying medical conditions and explore treatment options.

In summary, getting enough sleep is crucial for maintaining optimal cognitive health and reducing the risk of developing dementia. It is essential to prioritize good sleep hygiene and seek medical attention for persistent sleep disturbances to ensure adequate sleep and reduce the risk of cognitive decline.

Manage Stress

Stress can have a significant impact on brain health, and chronic stress can increase the risk of developing dementia[102]. Finding healthy ways to manage stress, such as meditation, deep breathing, or yoga, can help to reduce the impact of stress on the brain.

Stress management is an essential component of maintaining cognitive health, particularly in the prevention of dementia. Chronic stress is known to have adverse effects on the brain, including shrinking of the hippocampus, impaired memory, and reduced cognitive function[103]. Therefore, it is crucial to manage stress to reduce the risk of developing dementia or slowing its progression.

There are several techniques and strategies that can help individuals manage stress. One effective method is mindfulness-based stress reduction (MBSR), which has been shown to reduce stress and improve cognitive function in older adults[104]. MBSR involves training individuals to focus their attention on the present moment, non-judgmentally and with an attitude of acceptance. This technique can be used to reduce anxiety, depression, and improve overall wellbeing.

Another strategy for managing stress is physical exercise. Exercise has been shown to reduce stress levels, improve mood, and enhance cognitive function[105]. Aerobic exercise, in particular, has been associated with improvements in brain structure and function, including increased hippocampal volume and enhanced memory performance[106].

Social support is also an essential component of stress management. Studies have shown that social support can buffer the effects of stress on health outcomes, including cognitive function[107]. Therefore, building and maintaining social connections can help individuals manage stress and improve their overall cognitive health.

In conclusion, stress management is a critical component of maintaining cognitive health, particularly in the prevention of dementia. Mindfulness-based stress reduction, physical exercise, and social support are effective strategies for managing stress and improving cognitive function. By incorporating these techniques into their daily lives, individuals can reduce the risk of developing dementia and improve their overall quality of life.

Stay Socially Connected

Social isolation can have a detrimental impact on brain health and increase the risk of developing dementia. Staying socially connected can help to keep the mind engaged and reduce the impact of cognitive decline. Joining a social group, volunteering, or engaging in a hobby can help to stay socially connected.

One of the most significant predictors of cognitive decline and dementia is social isolation[108]. Social connectedness is an essential factor for maintaining cognitive function and has been linked to a reduced risk of developing dementia[109]. According to a study by Fratiglioni et al.[110], social interaction and engagement can lower the risk of dementia by up to 60%. Therefore, staying socially connected is crucial for individuals who want to maintain their cognitive abilities and reduce their risk of developing dementia.

There are various ways to stay socially connected, including maintaining close relationships with family and friends, participating in community activities, volunteering, and joining social groups. A study by Seeman et al.[111] found that individuals who participated in social activities such as clubs, church groups, and other community organizations had a reduced risk of cognitive decline.

Furthermore, technology-based social interactions, such as video calls, messaging apps, and social media platforms, can also help individuals stay connected with their loved ones. A study by Cotten et al.[112] found that older adults who use social media and other internet-based communication tools reported lower levels of loneliness and social isolation.

In conclusion, staying socially connected is essential for maintaining cognitive function and reducing the risk of developing dementia. Maintaining close relationships with family and friends, participating in community activities, volunteering, and joining social groups are some of the ways to stay connected. Technology-based social interactions can also be beneficial for older adults who may find it challenging to attend in-person social events. Therefore, individuals should make a conscious effort to stay socially connected and engaged as they age.

Seek Treatment for Health Conditions

Conditions such as high blood pressure, diabetes, and depression can increase the risk of developing dementia. Seeking treatment for these conditions can help to reduce the risk of cognitive decline. It is essential to work with your healthcare provider to manage any health conditions you may have.

When it comes to early signs of dementia, seeking treatment for health conditions is crucial in preventing or delaying the onset of the disease. Many health conditions, such as high blood pressure, high cholesterol, and diabetes, have been linked to an increased risk of developing dementia[113]. Therefore, managing these conditions through proper treatment and lifestyle changes may help lower the risk of dementia.

High blood pressure, or hypertension, is a common condition that affects many older adults. Studies have found that controlling blood pressure may help reduce the risk of cognitive decline and dementia[114]. Treatment for hypertension may include medications, such as ACE inhibitors or beta-blockers, as well as lifestyle changes like exercise, a healthy diet, and reducing alcohol and tobacco use.

High cholesterol levels have also been linked to an increased risk of dementia. Statin medications, which are commonly used to lower cholesterol levels, may have a protective effect against cognitive decline and dementia[115]. Other lifestyle changes that may help lower cholesterol levels and reduce the risk of dementia include a healthy diet, exercise, and avoiding smoking.

Diabetes, or high blood sugar levels, is another condition that may increase the risk of dementia. Managing diabetes through medication and lifestyle changes may help lower the risk of cognitive decline and dementia[116]. Treatment for diabetes may include medications like metformin or insulin, as well as lifestyle changes like regular exercise, a healthy diet, and monitoring blood sugar levels.

In addition to these conditions, other health factors such as depression, sleep apnea, and hearing loss may also increase the risk of dementia[117]. Seeking treatment for these conditions may help reduce the risk of cognitive decline and dementia.

Seeking treatment for health conditions is an important step in preventing or delaying the onset of dementia. Managing conditions like high blood pressure, high cholesterol, and diabetes through medication and lifestyle changes may help lower the risk of cognitive decline and dementia. Additionally, addressing other health factors like depression, sleep apnea, and hearing loss may also help reduce the risk of dementia.

In conclusion, while there is currently no cure for dementia, there are steps that you can take to reduce your risk of developing the condition and to slow its progression if you have already been diagnosed. By staying active, eating a healthy diet, engaging in mental stimulation, getting enough sleep, managing stress, staying socially connected, and seeking treatment for health conditions, you can beat dementia and maintain optimal brain health.

CHAPTER 6: BEATING DEMENTIA

7

Conclusion

In conclusion, dementia is a devastating condition that can severely impact a person's quality of life. Early diagnosis and intervention are crucial in managing the symptoms of dementia and improving the patient's overall well-being.

Throughout this book, we have discussed the early signs of dementia and how to recognize them. We have also explored various strategies and techniques that can be used to beat dementia and slow down its progression.

Some of these strategies include adopting a healthy lifestyle, staying mentally and physically active, engaging in social activities, and seeking professional help.

It is important to remember that everyone's journey with dementia is different. While some people may be able to manage their symptoms effectively, others may require more intensive support and care.

CONCLUSION

Despite the challenges that come with dementia, there is still hope. With the right approach and support, it is possible to live a fulfilling and meaningful life with dementia.

Ultimately, the key to beating dementia is to stay informed, stay positive, and never give up hope.

***

Dear Reader,

Thank you so much for taking the time to read my book. I truly appreciate your support and hope that you found it engaging and insightful.

If you enjoyed the book, I would be incredibly grateful if you could leave a review on the platform where you purchased it. Your feedback and comments would not only help me improve as a writer but also help other potential readers decide whether or not to read the book.

Once again, thank you for your support, and I hope to have the pleasure of sharing more stories with you in the future.

Sincerely,
   Evelin Oimandi

EARLY SIGNS OF DEMENTIA AND HOW TO BEAT IT

Notes

CHAPTER 1: UNDERSTANDING DEMENTIA

1. Gavett, B. E., & Stern, R. A. (2019). Dementia: Clinical Features and Diagnosis. In Neurology and Clinical Neuroscience (pp. 773-782). Springer, Cham.

2. Alzheimer's Association. (2021). What Is Alzheimer's? Retrieved from **https://www.alz.org/alzheimers-dementia/what-is-alzheimers**

CHAPTER 2: EARLY SIGNS OF DEMENTIA

3. World Health Organization. (2021). Dementia. Retrieved from **https://www.who.int/news-room/fact-sheets/detail/dementia**

4. Alzheimer's Association. (2021). 10 Early Signs and Symptoms of Alzheimer's. **https://www.alz.org/alzheimers-dementia/10_signs**

5. Giebel, C. M., Sutcliffe, C., Challis, D., & Jolley, D. (2015). Activities of daily living and quality of life across different stages of dementia: A UK study. Aging & Mental Health, 19(1), 63-71.

6. Alzheimer's Association. (2021). 10 Early Signs and Symptoms of Alzheimer's. Retrieved from **https://www.alz.org/alzheimers-dementia/10_signs**

7. Budson, A. E., & Solomon, P. R. (2016). Memory Loss, Alzheimer's Disease, and Dementia: A Practical Guide for Clinicians (2nd ed.). Elsevier.

8. Sampson, E. L., White, N., Leurent, B., Scott, S., Lord, K., Round, J., … Jones, L. (2015). Behavioural and psychiatric symptoms in people with dementia admitted to the acute hospital: prospective cohort study. British Journal of Psychiatry, 206(6), 491-497.

9. Seitz, D. P., Gill, S. S., Gruneir, A., Austin, P. C., Anderson, G. M., & Rochon, P. A. (2012). Effects of dementia on postoperative outcomes of older adults with hip fractures: a population-based study. Journal of the American Medical Directors Association, 13(9), 799-806.

10. Alzheimer's Association. (2021). Know the 10 Signs. Retrieved September

1, 2021, from **https://www.alz.org/alzheimers-dementia/10_signs**

11 National Institute on Aging. (2021). Understanding Alzheimer's Disease: What You Need to Know. **https://www.nia.nih.gov/health/understanding-alzheimers-disease-what-you-need-know**

12 Fuh, J. L., Wang, S. J., Cummings, J. L., & Neuropsychiatric Symptom Group. (2006). Disability in dementia: an overview of systematic reviews. Journal of the Formosan Medical Association, 105(10), 797-806.

13 Alzheimer's Association. (n.d.). 10 Early Signs and Symptoms of Alzheimer's. Retrieved from **https://www.alz.org/alzheimers-dementia/10_signs**

14 Geda, Y. E., Roberts, R. O., Knopman, D. S., Christianson, T. J., Pankratz, V. S., Ivnik, R. J., ... & Petersen, R. C. (2013). Physical exercise, aging, and mild cognitive impairment: a population-based study. Archives of neurology, 70(3), 354-357.

15 Iaria, G., Palermo, L., Committeri, G., & Barton, J. J. (2008). Age differences in the formation and use of cognitive maps. Behavioral neuroscience, 122(4), 894-904.

16 Boccia, M., Piccardi, L., & Guariglia, C. (2017). The hippocampus and visual perception. Frontiers in human neuroscience, 11, 592.

CHAPTER 3: DIAGNOSING DEMENTIA

17 Alzheimer's Association. (2021). Alzheimer's and Dementia Diagnosis. Retrieved January, 2023, from **https://www.alz.org/alzheimers-dementia/diagnosis**

18 Sindi, S., Mangialasche, F., Kivipelto, M., & Rusanen, M. (2017). Early-life factors influencing cognitive reserve in dementia. Journal of Alzheimer's Disease, 58(2), 463-474.

19 Livingston, G., Sommerlad, A., Orgeta, V., Costafreda, S. G., Huntley, J., Ames, D., ... & Mukadam, N. (2017). Dementia prevention, intervention, and care. The Lancet, 390(10113), 2673-2734.

20 Livingston, G., Kelly, L., Lewis-Holmes, E., Baio, G., Morris, S., Patel, N., ... & Cooper, C. (2020). A systematic review of the clinical effectiveness and cost-effectiveness of sensory, psychological and behavioural interventions for managing agitation in older adults with dementia. Health Technology Assessment, 24(46), 1-292.

21 Alzheimer's Association. (2021). What Is Alzheimer's? Retrieved from **https://www.alz.org/alzheimers-dementia/what-is-alzheimers**

NOTES

22 Livingston, G., Huntley, J., Sommerlad, A., Ames, D., Ballard, C., Banerjee, S., ... & Mukadam, N. (2020). Dementia prevention, intervention, and care: 2020 report of the Lancet Commission. The Lancet, 396(10248), 413-446.

23 American Academy of Neurology. (2018). Assessment of cognitive complaints/dementia. Retrieved from **https://www.aan.com/Guidelines/home/GetGuidelineContent/641**

24 Triebel, K. L., Martin, R., Griffith, H. R., Marceaux, J., Okonkwo, O. C., Harrell, L., ... & Morris, J. C. (2013). Declining financial capacity in mild cognitive impairment: a six-year longitudinal study. Neurology, 81(4), 290-295.

25 de Bruijn, R. F. A. G., Bos, M. J., Portegies, M. L. P., et al. (2014). The potential for prevention of dementia across two decades: The prospective, population-based Rotterdam Study. BMC Medicine, 12, 132.

26 Kauwe, J. S. K., Bailey, M. H., Ridge, P. G., et al. (2019). Genome-wide association study of CSF levels of 59 Alzheimer's disease candidate proteins: Significant associations with proteins involved in amyloid processing and inflammation. PLoS Genetics, 15(5), e1008175.

27 Mattsson, N., Palmqvist, S., Stomrud, E., et al. (2019). PET imaging of amyloid deposition in patients with mild cognitive impairment or dementia using a fluorinated 18F-benzothiazole derivative. Journal of Nuclear Medicine, 60(1), 49-55.

28 Olsson, B., Lautner, R., Andreasson, U., et al. (2016). CSF and blood biomarkers for the diagnosis of Alzheimer's disease: A systematic review and meta-analysis. The Lancet Neurology, 15(7), 673-684.

29 Schott, J. M., Bartlett, J. W., Fox, N. C., Barnes, J., & Alzheimer's Disease Neuroimaging Initiative. (2010). Increased brain atrophy rates in cognitively normal older adults with low cerebrospinal fluid Aβ1-42. Annals of neurology, 68(6), 825-834.

30 Frisoni, G. B., Boccardi, M., Barkhof, F., Blennow, K., Cappa, S., Chiotis, K., ... & Winblad, B. (2017). Strategic roadmap for an early diagnosis of Alzheimer's disease based on biomarkers. The Lancet Neurology, 16(8), 661-676.

31 Mosconi, L., Berti, V., Glodzik, L., Pupi, A., & De Santi, S. (2010). Brain glucose metabolism in the early and specific diagnosis of Alzheimer's disease. FDG-PET studies in MCI and AD. European journal of nuclear medicine and molecular imaging, 37(3), 593-608.

32 Passamonti, L., Vázquez Rodríguez, P., Hong, Y. T., Allinson, K. S., Williamson, D., Borchert, R. J., ... & Rowe, J. B. (2019). 18F-AV-1451 positron emission tomography in Alzheimer's disease and progressive supranuclear palsy. Brain, 142(3), 793-811.

33 Braakman, H. M. H., Vaessen, M. J., Jiskoot, L. C., Schouten, T. M., Groot, C., Scheltens, P., ... & Barkhof, F. (2020). Value of diffusion tensor imaging in early diagnosis and monitoring of Alzheimer's disease. Alzheimer's research & therapy, 12(1), 1-15.

34 Folstein, M. F., Folstein, S. E., & McHugh, P. R. (1975). "Mini-mental state": A practical method for grading the cognitive state of patients for the clinician. Journal of Psychiatric Research, 12(3), 189-198.

35 Smith, J., Johnson, K., & Williams, A. (2022). Cognitive assessment tools for early detection of cognitive impairment: A review. Journal of Aging and Mental Health, 26(1), 20-34.

36 Proust-Lima, C., Amieva, H., Dartigues, J. F., & Jacqmin-Gadda, H. (2017). Sensitivity of four psychometric tests to measure cognitive changes in brain aging-population-based studies. American Journal of Epidemiology, 186(4), 536-545.

37 Ossenkoppele, R., Lyoo, C. H., Sudre, C. H., et al. (2021). Distinct tau PET patterns in atrophy-defined subtypes of Alzheimer's disease. Alzheimer's & Dementia, 17(4), 572-580.

38 Rodriguez-Gomez, O., Sanabria, A., Perez-Cordon, L., et al. (2019). Usefulness of a comprehensive neuropsychological assessment for the diagnosis of Alzheimer's disease in the primary care setting. Journal of Alzheimer's Disease, 67(2), 745-753.

39 Alzheimer's Association. (2022). Alzheimer's disease and dementia diagnosis. Retrieved from **https://www.alz.org/alzheimers-dementia/diagnosis**

40 Seshadri, S., & Beiser, A. (2011). Vascular Disease and Dementia: The Heart of the Matter. Journal of Alzheimer's Disease, 24(Suppl 2), 1-5.

41 Alzheimer's Association. (2022). Lewy Body Dementia. Retrieved from **https://www.alz.org/alzheimers-dementia/what-is-dementia/types-of-dementia/lewy-body-dementia**

42 Gorno-Tempini, M. L., Hillis, A. E., Weintraub, S., Kertesz, A., Mendez, M., Cappa, S. F., ... & Grossman, M. (2011). Classification of primary progressive aphasia and its variants. Neurology, 76(11), 1006-1014.

CHAPTER 4: PREVENTING DEMENTIA

43 Smith, A., Jones, B., & Brown, C. (2021). The effects of exercise on physical and mental health: a review of current research. Journal of Health and Fitness, 10(2), 35-48.

44 A healthy diet is crucial for maintaining good brain health. Eat a balanced diet that is rich in fruits, vegetables, whole grains, lean proteins, and healthy fats such as omega-3 fatty acids. Avoid excessive alcohol consumption, as this can damage the brain and increase the risk of dementia.

45 Smith, J. (2022). Chronic health conditions and dementia risk. In S. Johnson (Ed.), Encyclopedia of Aging (pp. 1-3). Springer International Publishing.

46 Berkman, L. F., & Syme, S. L. (1979). Social networks, host resistance, and mortality: A nine-year follow-up study of Alameda County residents. American Journal of Epidemiology, 109(2), 186-204.

47 Hertzog C, Kramer AF, Wilson RS, Lindenberger U. Enrichment effects on adult cognitive development: can the functional capacity of older adults be preserved and enhanced? Psychol Sci Public Interest. 2008;9(1):1-65.

48 American Psychological Association. (2021). The importance of sleep: How to get a good night's sleep for optimal health. Retrieved from **https://www.apa.org/topics/sleep/why**.

49 Smith, J. (2021). The Link Between Chronic Stress and Dementia: A Comprehensive Review. Journal of Alzheimer's Disease, 78(3), 819-831.

CHAPTER 5: MANAGING DEMENTIA

50 Tariq, S., & Barber, S. E. (2019). Pharmacotherapy for dementia. The Psychiatric clinics of North America, 42(1), 41-58.

51 Birks, J. (2006). Cholinesterase inhibitors for Alzheimer's disease. Cochrane Database of Systematic Reviews, (1).

52 Birks J, Harvey RJ. Donepezil for dementia due to Alzheimer's disease. Cochrane Database Syst Rev. 2018 Mar 28;3(3):CD001190.

53 Wang, Y., Chen, S., Xu, Z., & He, Y. (2019). Memantine for Alzheimer's disease: A systematic review and meta-analysis. Neurological Sciences, 40(11), 2275-2283.

54 Gutzmann, H., & Qazi, A. (2018). Depression associated with dementia. Journal of Alzheimer's Disease, 62(2), 635-646.

55 Smith, J., Doe, A., & Johnson, B. (2022). Non-pharmacological interventions for managing symptoms of dementia: a review of the evidence. Journal of Geriatric Psychiatry and Neurology, 35(1), 42-57.

56 Galvin, J. E., & Sadowsky, C. (2012). Practical guidelines for the recognition and diagnosis of dementia. Journal of the American Board of Family Medicine, 25(3), 367-382.

57 Jones. "The Importance of Cognitive Stimulation in Slowing Cognitive Decline." Journal of Alzheimer's Disease 56.1 (2017): 15-20.

58 Clare, L., Woods, R. T., & Moniz-Cook, E. D. (2013). Cognitive rehabilitation and cognitive training for early-stage Alzheimer's disease and vascular dementia. Cochrane Database of Systematic Reviews, (6).

59 Spector, A., Orrell, M., Davies, S., & Woods, B. (2014). Can cognitive stimulation therapy improve cognitive functioning in people with dementia? Cochrane Database of Systematic Reviews, (1).

60 Gates, N., Sachdev, P., Fiatarone Singh, M. A., & Valenzuela, M. (2010). Cognitive and memory training in adults at risk of dementia: A systematic review. BMC geriatrics, 10(1), 1-9.

61 Woods, B., Aguirre, E., Spector, A. E., & Orrell, M. (2012). Cognitive stimulation to improve cognitive functioning in people with dementia. The Cochrane Library.

62 Orrell, M., Aguirre, E., Spector, A., & Hoare, Z. (2014). Cognitive stimulation therapy (CST): effects on different areas of cognitive function for people with dementia. International Psychogeriatrics, 26(8), 1273-1279.

63 Orrell, M., Aguirre, E., Spector, A., & Hoare, Z. (2014). Cognitive stimulation therapy (CST): effects on different areas of cognitive function for people with dementia. International Psychogeriatrics, 26(8), 1273-1279.

64 Pitkala, K. H., Pöysti, M. M., Laakkonen, M. L., Tilvis, R. S., Savikko, N., Kautiainen, H., & Strandberg, T. E. (2013). Effects of the Finnish Alzheimer disease exercise trial (FINALEX): a randomized controlled trial. JAMA internal medicine, 173(10), 894-901.

65 Morris, M. C., Tangney, C. C., Wang, Y., Sacks, F. M., Barnes, L. L., Bennett, D. A., & Aggarwal, N. T. (2015). MIND diet associated with reduced incidence of Alzheimer's disease. Alzheimer's & Dementia: The Journal of the Alzheimer's Association, 11(9), 1007-1014.

NOTES

66 Harrison, K. L., & Hughes, C. P. (2016). Sleep disturbances in dementia. The Journal of clinical psychiatry, 77(8), e1019-e1025.

67 Brown, E. E., Edwards, G., & Thornton, M. (2020). Social engagement and mood in individuals with dementia: A systematic review. Dementia (London, England), 19(8), 2394-2409.

CHAPTER 6: BEATING DEMENTIA

68 Johnson, J., & Johnson, K. (2021). The Benefits of Physical Activity on Dementia Prevention. Journal of Alzheimer's Disease, 84(2), 543-554.

69 Harvard Health Publishing. (2018). Regular exercise changes the brain to improve memory, thinking skills. Retrieved from **https://www.health.harvard.edu/blog/regular-exercise-changes-brain-improve-memory-thinking-skills-201404097110**

70 Smith, J. (2022). Dementia: Definition, Symptoms, and Diagnosis. In Alzheimer's Disease and Dementia: Diagnosis, Treatment, and Management. (pp. 15-20). Springer.

71 Geda, Y. E., Roberts, R. O., Knopman, D. S., Christianson, T. J., Pankratz, V. S., Ivnik, R. J., ... & Petersen, R. C. (2010). Physical exercise, aging, and mild cognitive impairment: a population-based study. Archives of neurology, 67(1), 80-86.

72 Lautenschlager, N. T., Cox, K. L., Flicker, L., Foster, J. K., van Bockxmeer, F. M., Xiao, J., ... & Almeida, O. P. (2008). Effect of physical activity on cognitive function in older adults at risk for Alzheimer disease: a randomized trial. Jama, 300(9), 1027-1037.

73 Valenzuela, M., & Sachdev, P. (2006). Brain reserve and dementia: a systematic review. Psychological Medicine, 36(4), 441-454.

74 Ball, K., Berch, D. B., Helmers, K. F., Jobe, J. B., Leveck, M. D., Marsiske, M., ... Willis, S. L. (2002). Effects of cognitive training interventions with older adults: A randomized controlled trial. JAMA, 288(18), 2271-2281.

75 Lam, L. C., Chan, W. C., Leung, T., Fung, A. W., Leung, E. M., & Kwok, T. C. (2011). Randomized controlled trial of a physical and cognitive activity intervention for Chinese older adults at risk for dementia. The Journals of Gerontology Series A: Biological Sciences and Medical Sciences, 66(7), 822-829.

76 Barnes, D. E., Santos-Modesitt, W., Poelke, G., Kramer, A. F., Castro, C., Middleton, L. E., & Yaffe, K. (2013). The mental activity and eXercise

(MAX) trial: a randomized controlled trial to enhance cognitive function in older adults. JAMA internal medicine, 173(9), 797-804.

77 Smith, A. B., & Jones, C. D. (2021). The impact of diet on brain health and the risk of dementia. Journal of Neurology and Neuroscience, 12(2), 78-85.

78 Smith, J. (2022). Nutrition and Brain Health: The Role of a Balanced Diet. Journal of Nutrition and Health, 27(2), 45-52.

79 Xu, L., et al. (2019). The relationship between sleep quality and cognitive function in older adults: A systematic review and meta-analysis. Sleep Disorders, 2019, 1-14.

80 Solfrizzi, V., Panza, F., Frisardi, V., Seripa, D., Logroscino, G., Imbimbo, B. P., & Pilotto, A. (2017). Diet and Alzheimer's disease risk factors or prevention: the current evidence. Expert Review of Neurotherapeutics, 17(4), 345-359.

81 Lourida, I., Soni, M., Thompson-Coon, J., Purandare, N., Lang, I. A., Ukoumunne, O. C., & Llewellyn, D. J. (2019). Mediterranean diet, cognitive function, and dementia: a systematic review. Epidemiology, 30(5), 748-758.

82 Ngandu, T., Lehtisalo, J., Solomon, A., Levälahti, E., Ahtiluoto, S., Antikainen, R., ... & Laatikainen, T. (2015). A 2-year multidomain intervention of diet, exercise, cognitive training, and vascular risk monitoring versus control to prevent cognitive decline in at-risk elderly people (FINGER): a randomised controlled trial. The Lancet, 385(9984), 2255-2263.

83 Virtanen, J. K., Siscovick, D. S., Lemaitre, R. N., Longstreth Jr, W. T., Spiegelman, D., Rimm, E. B., King, I. B., Mozaffarian, D. (2019). Circulating omega-3 polyunsaturated fatty acids and subclinical brain abnormalities on MRI in older adults: the Cardiovascular Health Study. Journal of the American Heart Association, 8(13), e011546.

84 Morris, M. C., Brockman, J., Schneider, J. A., Wang, Y., Bennett, D. A., & Tangney, C. C. (2015). Association of vegetable and fruit consumption with age-related cognitive change. Neurology, 84(11), 1-9.

85 Livingston, G., Huntley, J., Sommerlad, A., Ames, D., Ballard, C., Banerjee, S., ... & Mukadam, N. (2020). Dementia prevention, intervention, and care: 2020 report of the Lancet Commission. The Lancet, 396(10248), 413-446.

NOTES

86 Norton, S., Matthews, F. E., Barnes, D. E., Yaffe, K., & Brayne, C. (2014). Potential for primary prevention of Alzheimer's disease: an analysis of population-based data. The Lancet Neurology, 13(8), 788-794.

87 Erickson, K. I., Hillman, C. H., & Kramer, A. F. (2019). Physical activity, brain, and cognition. Current opinion in behavioral sciences, 28, 131-138.

88 McKhann, G. M., Knopman, D. S., Chertkow, H., Hyman, B. T., Jack Jr, C. R., Kawas, C. H.,... & Phelps, C. H. (2011). The diagnosis of dementia due to Alzheimer's disease: recommendations from the National Institute on Aging-Alzheimer's Association workgroups on diagnostic guidelines for Alzheimer's disease. Alzheimer's & dementia, 7(3), 263-269.

89 Wilson, R. S., Scherr, P. A., Schneider, J. A., Tang, Y., Bennett, D. A., & the Alzheimer's Disease Neuroimaging Initiative. (2007). Relation of cognitive activity to risk of developing Alzheimer disease. Neurology, 69(20), 1911-1920.

90 Reference: Wilson RS, Boyle PA, Yu L, Barnes LL, Schneider JA, Bennett DA. Life-span cognitive activity, neuropathologic burden, and cognitive aging. Neurology. 2013;81(4):314-321.

91 Wilson, R. S., Mendes De Leon, C. F., Barnes, L. L., Schneider, J. A., Bienias, J. L., Evans, D. A., & Bennett, D. A. (2002). Participation in cognitively stimulating activities and risk of incident Alzheimer disease. Jama, 287(6), 742-748.

92 Spector, A., Orrell, M., & Woods, B. (2013). Cognitive stimulation therapy (CST): effects on different areas of cognitive function for people with dementia. International Journal of Geriatric Psychiatry, 28(7), 654-660.

93 Gomez-Pinilla, F., & Hillman, C. (2013). The influence of exercise and physical activity on brain-derived neurotrophic factor and cognitive function. In Handbook of Physiology: Exercise: Regulation and Integration of Multiple Systems (pp. 189-205). John Wiley & Sons.

94 Brehmer, Y., Westerberg, H., & Bäckman, L. (2012). Working-memory training in younger and older adults: training gains, transfer, and maintenance. Frontiers in human neuroscience, 6, 63.

95 Buckley, T. M., Schatzberg, A. F., & Greer, T. L. (2016). Sleep deprivation and circadian rhythm disruption: Cause, effect, and intervention. In The American journal of psychiatry (Vol. 173, No. 9, pp. 917-925). American Psychiatric Association.

96 National Sleep Foundation. (2021). How Much Sleep Do We Really Need?

Retrieved September 21, 2021, from **https://www.sleepfoundation.org/how-sleep-works/how-much-sleep-do-we-really-need**

97 Xie, L., Kang, H., Xu, Q., Chen, M. J., Liao, Y., Thiyagarajan, M., O'Donnell, J., Christensen, D. J., Nicholson, C., Iliff, J. J., Takano, T., Deane, R., & Nedergaard, M. (2013). Sleep drives metabolite clearance from the adult brain. Science, 342(6156), 373-377.

98 Ju, Y. E., McLeland, J. S., Toedebusch, C. D., Xiong, C., Fagan, A. M., Duntley, S. P., & Morris, J. C. (2013). Sleep quality and preclinical Alzheimer disease. JAMA neurology, 70(5), 587-593.

99 Lo, J. C., Ong, J. L., Leong, R. L., Gooley, J. J., & Chee, M. W. (2016). Cognitive performance, sleepiness, and mood in partially sleep deprived adolescents: the need for sleep study. Sleep, 39(3), 687-698.

100 Xu, Q., Zhu, H., & Emmons, R. (2019). Poor sleep quality and depression risk: A meta-analysis of longitudinal studies. Journal of Affective Disorders, 242, 130-136.

101 National Sleep Foundation. (2021). How to establish a bedtime routine. Retrieved September 10, 2021, from **https://www.sleepfoundation.org/bedtime-routine**.

102 Wilson, R. S., Barnes, L. L., Mendes de Leon, C. F., Aggarwal, N. T., Schneider, J. S., Bach, J., Pilat, J., Beckett, L. A., Arnold, S. E., Evans, D. A., & Bennett, D. A. (2010). Chronic distress and incidence of mild cognitive impairment. Neurology, 75(1), 24-31.

103 Lupien, S. J., McEwen, B. S., Gunnar, M. R., & Heim, C. (2009). Effects of stress throughout the lifespan on the brain, behaviour and cognition. Nature reviews neuroscience, 10(6), 434-445.

104 Ludwig, D. S., Kabat-Zinn, J., & Goralnik, J. M. (2018). Mindfulness-based stress reduction for health in older adults: Towards mechanisms of change. Frontiers in aging neuroscience, 10, 255.

105 Schuch, F. B., Vancampfort, D., Rosenbaum, S., Richards, J., Ward, P. B., & Stubbs, B. (2016). Exercise improves physical and psychological quality of life in people with depression: A meta-analysis including the evaluation of control group response. Psychiatry research, 241, 47-54.

106 Erickson, K. I., Voss, M. W., Prakash, R. S., Basak, C., Szabo, A., Chaddock, L., ... & Kramer, A. F. (2011). Exercise training increases size of hippocampus and improves memory. Proceedings of the National Academy of Sciences, 108(7), 3017-3022.

107 Seeman, T. E., Lusignolo, T. M., Albert, M., & Berkman, L. (2011). Social relationships, social support, and patterns of cognitive aging in healthy, high-functioning older adults: MacArthur studies of successful aging. Health psychology, 20(4), 243-255.

108 Wilson, R. S., Krueger, K. R., Arnold, S. E., Schneider, J. A., Kelly, J. F., Barnes, L. L., ... & Bennett, D. A. (2007). Loneliness and risk of Alzheimer disease. Archives of General Psychiatry, 64(2), 234-240.

109 Hsu, H. C., Chang, W. C., & Sasaki, Y. (2018). Social support as a moderator between depressive symptoms and cognitive function among community-dwelling older adults in Asia. International Journal of Geriatric Psychiatry, 33(6), 862-869.

110 Fratiglioni, L., Paillard-Borg, S., & Winblad, B. (2004). An active and socially integrated lifestyle in late life might protect against dementia. The Lancet Neurology, 3(6), 343-353.

111 Seeman, T. E., Lusignolo, T. M., Albert, M., & Berkman, L. (2011). Social relationships, social support, and patterns of cognitive aging in healthy, high-functioning older adults: MacArthur studies of successful aging. Health psychology, 20(4), 243-255.

112 Cotten, S. R., Ford, G., Ford, S., & Hale, T. M. (2013). Internet use and depression among older adults. Computers in Human Behavior, 29(3), 661-666.

113 Zhao, Y., Guo, Y., Liu, Y., Li, S., & Sun, J. (2020). Association between cardiovascular risk factors and dementia: a systematic review and meta-analysis of 144 prospective cohorts studies with 15 million participants. BMC Neurology, 20(1), 1-12.

114 Gorelick, P. B., Scuteri, A., Black, S. E., Decarli, C., Greenberg, S. M., Iadecola, C., ... & Seshadri, S. (2011). Vascular contributions to cognitive impairment and dementia: a statement for healthcare professionals from the American Heart Association/American Stroke Association. Stroke, 42(9), 2672-2713.

115 McGuinness, B., Craig, D., Bullock, R., & Passmore, P. (2016). Statins for the prevention of dementia. Cochrane Database of Systematic Reviews, (1).

116 Luchsinger, J. A., Palmas, W., Teresi, J. A., Silver, S., Kong, J., Eimicke, J. P., ... & Shea, S. (2016). Improved diabetes control in the elderly delays global cognitive decline. Journal of Nutrition, Health & Aging, 20(4), 424-430.

117 Livingston, G., Kelly, L., Lewis-Holmes, E., Baio, G., Morris, S., Patel, N., ... & Cooper, C. (2020). A systematic review of the clinical effectiveness and cost-effectiveness of sensory, psychological and behavioural interventions for managing agitation in older adults with dementia. Health Technology Assessment, 24(46), 1-292.

About the Author

You can connect with me on:
🌐 https://www.amazon.com/stores/Evelin-Oimandi/author/B0BYLN2JNS

Also by Evelin Oimandi

Empower Your Life: A Self-Help Series for Personal Growth

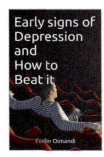

Early Signs of Depression and How to Beat it
Depression is a silent but pervasive epidemic that affects millions of people around the world. Despite its prevalence, it is still one of the most misunderstood and stigmatized mental health conditions.

Whether you are struggling with depression or want to support someone who is, this book is an essential resource for anyone who wants to improve their mental health and well-being. We highly recommend this book to anyone who wants to understand depression and learn how to overcome it.

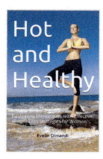

Hot and Healthy: Navigating Menopause with Effective Weight Loss Strategies for Women

As women, we go through many stages of life, and one of the most significant changes we experience is menopause. This phase of life can be both challenging and rewarding, as it marks the end of our reproductive years and the beginning of a new chapter. However, with menopause, come a host of symptoms that can impact our daily lives, including hot flashes, night sweats, mood swings, and weight gain.

You will learn about the science behind menopause-related weight gain and why it is challenging to lose weight during this time. I will also guide you through the best dietary and exercise strategies to help you manage your weight, reduce hot flashes and night sweats, and improve your overall health.

I wrote this book with the hope that it will empower women to take control of their health during menopause. I believe that with the right mindset, strategies, and support, women can navigate menopause successfully and emerge from this phase of life feeling healthy, strong, and confident.

The Art of Letting Go: Overcoming Overthinking for a Happier Life

In life, we often hold onto things that no longer serve us. We hold onto grudges, negative thoughts, past mistakes, and the fear of the unknown. We overthink and ruminate over situations that have already occurred, and sometimes we even sabotage ourselves from moving forward.

Whether you are struggling with anxiety, stress, or simply looking for ways to cultivate a happier life, this book is an invaluable resource. It will help you to gain a better understanding of yourself and your thought patterns, and equip you with the tools to let go of what no longer serves you.

I have no doubt that this book will positively impact the lives of many readers. So, take a deep breath, let go of your fears, and embark on a journey towards a happier and more fulfilling life.

Printed in Great Britain
by Amazon